3-5 84

THE MASSES
OF FRANCESCO SORIANO

Plate I. Francesco Soriano. Title page from *Missarum liber primus*.

THE MASSES

OF FRANCESCO SORIANO

A Style-Critical Study

by S. Philip Kniseley

UNIVERSITY OF FLORIDA PRESS / GAINESVILLE, 1967

COPYRIGHT © 1967 BY THE BOARD OF
COMMISSIONERS OF STATE INSTITUTIONS
OF FLORIDA

LIBRARY OF CONGRESS
CATALOG CARD No. 67-22198

PRINTED BY THE STORTER PRINTING COMPANY
GAINESVILLE, FLORIDA

INTRODUCTION

The name of Francesco Soriano came to the author's attention during his studies in the area of the late Renaissance. Soriano was a member of the circle of composers around, and greatly overshadowed by, Palestrina. The printed works of these minor figures lie forgotten for the most part in the archives of the churches and libraries of Italy and the rest of Europe.

Soriano's known works can be listed:

1581 *Il libro primo di madrigale a 5 voci.*
1592 *Il libro secondo di madrigale a 5 voci.*
1597 *Motectorum quae octo vocibus concinuntur, liber primus*
1602 *Il libro primo di madrigale a 4 voci.*
1609 *Missarum liber primus.*
1610 *Canoni et oblighi di 110 sorte, sopra l'Ave maris stella.*
1616 *Psalmi et motecta, quae octo, duodecim et sexdecim voci.*
1619 *Passio D. N. Jesu Christe secundum quatuor Evangelistas, Magnificat, Sexdecim; Sequentia fidelium Defunctorum, una cum Responsorio.*

To these can be added some fifteen secular pieces in various collections and five sacred pieces, most of which are found in the list of published volumes.

When this list is compared to the complete works of Soriano's contemporaries, such as Annibale Stabile, the Nanino brothers, the Anerio brothers, Ruggerio Giovanelli, Paolo Quagliata, and Giovanni Dragoni, Soriano's quantity is seen to be the same. These men were all devoted admirers of Palestrina, but it cannot be said that they were simply imitators, for they were all working in a medium that was modern and up-to-date in every respect.

Soriano's Mass book of 1609 was chosen for a style-critical study because it offers a comprehensive picture of his style over a possible twenty-two-year period. The author worked from a microfilm of the Mass book published by F. B. Robblettus in Rome, now located in the Vatican Library. The *Missarum liber primus* is a Mass book in large folio and follows the usual conventions of such publications: absence of bar lines, uniform length of parts on a page, white notation with occasional coloration, and rather frequent use of ligatures, mostly of the *cum opposita propietate* variety. The Masses are in *tempus imperfectum, diminutum* (₵) throughout; examples have been transposed to modern clefs and are reduced by one-half to the modern *alla breve*, but references to note-values in the text refer to the original. Plates III and IV are reproductions of the beginning of the Kyrie of the *Missa secundi toni.*

Word setting and modal practice in Soriano's Masses show no significant departure from common practice of the late Renaissance and therefore were omitted from this study.

This monograph was taken in part from the author's dissertation available at University Microfilms, Inc., Ann Arbor, Michigan, order No. 65-9032. Volume II of this dissertation (musical supplement) is a transcription of the Masses into modern notation. The eight Masses are:

I	*Missa nos autem gloriari, a 4.*
II	*Missa ad canones, a 4.*
III	*Missa sine titulo, a 5.*
IV	*Missa Quando laeta sperabam, a 5.*
V	*Missa octavi toni, a 5.*
VI	*Missa secundi toni, a 6.*
VII	*Missa super voces musicales, a 6.*
VIII	*Missa in Papae Marcelli, a 8.*

CONTENTS

1. BIOGRAPHY

Francesco Soriano (1549-c.1621) was born in the district of Viterbo in the town of Soriano, north of Rome, which at the time was part of the papal states.[1] The date of his birth is derived from a medallion portrait on the title page of one of his last published works (Plate II), and the place of his birth is given in the preface to *Libro quatro delle Messe in spartitura* by Paolo Agostini in 1627. Agostini was Soriano's second successor as *maestro di cappella* at St. Peter's in Rome and speaks in glowing terms of Soriano's ability as a composer. Agostini also came from the Viterbo district.

Most biographical information on the life and works of Soriano comes from Giuseppe Baini[2] and Francis Haberl,[3] and later writers appear to get most of their information from these two sources. Haberl gives the most accurate information, for he uses not only Baini but also letters from contemporary sources, prefaces to published works, and archive material from various Roman and Mantuan sources.

Baini states that Soriano at the age of fifteen entered the choir of St. John Lateran in Rome where he received his first instruction in music from Annibale Zoilo and Bartholomo Roy. This would be in the year 1564, and immediately the question arises as to why he would be admitted after the age at which natural mutation of the voice has normally taken place. There is no suggestion anywhere that he was a castrato singer. Baini remarks that when Soriano's voice changed, he was given further instruction by Giovanni Battista Montenare.[4] It is possible that he entered the choir as a male alto or falsettist and then lost his voice.

Baini next places him in the school of Giovanni Maria Nanino, where he also came under the direction of Pierluigi da Palestrina.

1. Other variants of spelling include Suriani, Suriano, Surianus, and Sorianus. After he took up permanent residence in Rome in 1587, he added the name of that city to his own, perhaps reflecting his pride at being considered a "Roman." Variant spellings include Romano, Romani, and Romanus.

2. Giuseppe Baini, *Memorie storico—Critiche della vita e delle opere di Giovanni Pierluigi da Palestrina* (Rome, 1828).

3. Francis Haberl, "Lebensgang und Werke des Francesco Soriano," *Kirchenmusikalisches Jahrbuch*, X (1895), 95-103.

4. Baini, *op. cit.*, II, 30.

There is no documentary evidence that this is factual, except that Palestrina himself later names him as a student in a letter to the Duke of Mantua. The first time Soriano's name appears in print is in *Quatro libro delle muse*, a collection published in 1574. Other composers represented in this collection are Giovanni Animuccia, Palestrina, G. M. Nanino, Giovanni Maque, Rosselo, A. Zoilo, N. Perve, G. A. Dragoni, Rodolfo Pierluigi (son of Palestrina), Giovanni Troiani, and Bartholomo Roy. The presence of Palestrina, Nanino, Palestrina's son Rodolfo, and the two known students of Palestrina, Soriano and Dragoni, gives this publication the appearance of a school collection. Soriano's contribution to the book is a madrigal *a 5* titled "Caddi al primo apparir."

The date 1574 helps account for another period in Soriano's life. It is known that he was ordained as a priest and served in the parish of Rome, so his seminary training would fit into the years 1564-74, probably after his usefulness as a singer at St. John Lateran had come to an end.

The first independent publication of Soriano appeared in 1581,[5] and in the preface he calls himself *maestro di cappella* of St. Luigi, the French national church in Rome. The dedication is to Guglielmo Gonzaga, Duke of Mantua, and apparently pleased the Duke, for that same year finds Soriano as *maestro di cappella* at the Mantuan court, a position which he held until 1586.[6] This first book was re-published by Croce in 1588, and in that preface Soriano writes that he is now *maestro* at Santa Maria Maggiore in Rome.

Soriano did not publish any independent works during his years at Mantua, but his name appears in several collections of madrigals. Then in 1585, a motet *a 8*, "In illo tempore," appears in Victoria's *Motecta festorum totius anni* along with a work by Guerrero. Haberl suggests that "Guerrero konnte gut der Lehrer des jungen Victoria gewesen sein, der Römer Soriano sicher ein guter Freund und Kunstgenosse."[7] This statement is apparently misunderstood by Pedrell, for he writes: "Haberl believes that Guerrero (1529-1599) was the teacher of the young Victoria and that Suriano (1545-1620) would perhaps be called his good friend and artistic professor. Should this mean that both were his teachers or both

---

5. *Il libro primo di madrigale a 5 voci* (Venezia: Gardano, 1581).
6. Haberl *op. cit.*, p. 96.
7. Haberl, "Thomas Luca Victoria," p. 79. Complete information on source materials may be found in the Bibliography.

were his artistic professors? There is really no justification for anyone putting such empty suppositions into print. One simply has to compare the second volume of [Victoria's] *Hispaniae Schola*, which is dedicated to Guerrero, with any composition taken from the life of Soriano and be convinced of the impossibility of such an assumption . . . the composition by Guerrero and that by the Roman composer Francisco Suriano were perhaps included simply to fill out the remaining pages."[8] It is apparent that Haberl meant no such thing, and Pedrell's interpretation of the word "Kunstgenosse" leads to his criticism. More important to us is that it suggests that Victoria and Soriano were seminary students together; Victoria was ordained in 1575.[9]

The period of employment at Mantua apparently was not entirely satisfactory, for in 1583 the Duke instructed his ambassador in Rome, Zibramonti, to see if a suitable replacement could be found. Zibramonti reported back by letter that he had asked Palestrina's advice on the matter. Palestrina said he could only recommend Zoilo who would not consider a change because of family problems. Marenzio was available, but Palestrina felt that he was no better as a music director or composer than Soriano. When Palestrina gave the impression that he might be interested in the position, the Duke inquired directly as to terms. Palestrina answered that he would dislike very much to take a position away from one of his pupils of whom he was quite fond. The terms he then put forth were such that the Duke had to decline.[10]

Soriano remained at his post until 1586, and when he left, the court records were most careful to emphasize that he left of his own accord. No successor was named to this position, and the duties of director and composer were taken over by singers already in the chapel.

Compositions by Soriano from this period are scarce. We have only one sacred work, the motet included by Victoria in his *Motecta festorum totius anni* of 1585. It could be reasonably assumed that Soriano's duties included a certain number of compositions for the Duke's chapel, but nothing was published. This is

8. Philippe Pedrell (ed.), *Thomas Ludivici Victoria: Opera Omnia*, xxxix, xli. Translation the author's; subsequent translations also the author's unless otherwise noted.

9. Gustave Reese, *Music in the Renaissance*, p. 599.

10. Haberl, "Das Archiv der Gonzaga in Mantua," p. 41.

3

understandable when we remember that the ten alternation Masses (alternating plainsong and polyphony) submitted to the Duke by Palestrina were never published but found their way into the Mantuan archives and remained there until discovered by Jeppesen.[11] Perhaps further investigation of these sources would add to the list of Soriano's works.

Soriano contributed the "Christe" *a 8* and "Et ascendit" *a 4* to the *Missa Cantantibus organus,* based on Palestrina's motet of the same name.[12] This Mass (mostly *a 12*) was a joint undertaking of Palestrina, Stabile, Dragoni, Giovanelli, Cruzio Mancini, Prospero Santini, and Soriano and was found in the archives of St. John Lateran.

In 1587 Soriano succeeded Nicolas Peruve at Santa Maria Maggiore in Rome as *maestro di cappella* of the Liberian chapel, for which he was paid four scudi per month; from this he had to provide for the care of four choir boys. During his eleven years there, single madrigal compositions appear in six madrigal collections. In 1592 Soriano's *Il secondo libro di madrigale a cinque voci* was printed by Francesco Coattini and is dedicated to Cardinal Scipio Gonzaga, Patriarch of Jerusalem and nephew of the Duke of Mantua. Thus Soriano seems to have maintained a friendly relationship with the house of Gonzaga. In this publication Soriano mentions Montenare as one of his teachers and includes one of his works. After the time of this publication Soriano adds "Romano" to his name, reflecting his attachment to the Eternal City.

In 1593 an event took place in Rome which helped establish Soriano as one of the foremost contrapuntalists of his time. A Spaniard, Sebastian Raval, arrived in Rome and quickly published three of his own works. He then announced that he was the best musician in the world and that all of Italy had never before seen the likes of him.[13] He was at once challenged to an extemporaneous contest in composition and was matched against G. M. Nanino and Francesco Soriano. As related by Baini, before Raval could figure out the opening measures, Nanino and Soriano had completed their compositions.

---

11. Knud Jeppesen, "The Recently Discovered Montova Masses of Palestrina," p. 36.
12. Raphael Casimiri (ed.), *Missa Cantantibus Organis.*
13. Baini, *op. cit.,* II, 39.

Another instance of Soriano's growing importance was his appointment, along with Dragoni, by the *Archiconfraternità della Santissima Trinità* to arbitrate a dispute over a fair pay-scale for the services rendered the fraternity by Asperilio Pacilli in 1595. The letter containing suggestions of Soriano and Dragoni is to be found in the Heyer-Museum in Cologne.[14] Soriano's first published volume of sacred music, *Motectorum quae octo vocibus concinuntur, liber primus*, appeared in 1597.

In 1599 Soriano accepted the position as *maestro di cappella* at St. John Lateran where he had served as a choir boy many years before. In 1601 he returned to Santa Maria Maggiore. In that year he published the first book of madrigals *a 4* dedicated to Cardinal Aldobrandini. Baini mentions a second book published the following year, but this has not been verified by any other source.[15]

In 1603 Soriano was named *maestro di cappella* at St. Peter's Basilica and remained there until his retirement in 1620 at the age of seventy-one. It was during this time that he published the major portion of his sacred works; only four more secular pieces appear during his latter years.

One of Soriano's first tasks upon assuming the duties at St. Peter's was to try to rectify a painful situation in its musical organization. Since 1597, Ercole Pasquini had been organist at the basilica, but illness made his execution of the office less than satisfactory. According to Haberl, the archive records of St. Peter's show that by 1605, the director of the insane asylum was drawing six scudi each month for the care of Pasquini, and in May of 1608, matters came to a head. The prefect of the music chapel, Canonicus Riccardelli, was instructed to remove with just cause the organist Hercules (Pasquini) from his position and forbid him to participate further in the service of the church.

An entry in the record shows that N. N. of Ferrara was elected organist. From May to November, Allesandro Costantini (the first runner-up) served as interim organist, and in November a contract beginning "Io Hieronymus Frescobaldi" and initialed "N. N." was deposited in the archives. It bound the organist to the post without leave, salary increase, or living allowance until the end of 1628. His beginning salary was six scudi a month. Soriano now had one of the most famous organists of all Europe under his direction.

14. Georg Kinsky, "Schriftstücke aus dem Palestrina Kreis," p. 114.
15. Baini, *op. cit.*, II, 30.

Plate II. Francesco Soriano. Title page from *Passio D. N. Jesu Christe secundum quatuor Evangelistas.*

The first major work published by Soriano while at St. Peter's was the *Missarum liber primus*, printed by J. B. Robblettus in 1609. The frontispiece has a picture of Soriano presenting the book to Pope Paul V, to whom the work is dedicated. This picture (Plate I) is not mentioned in any sources consulted and shows a traditional

6

pose seen in such works of the period. A comparison of the medallion portrait on the frontispiece of another of Soriano's works (Plate II) indicates that it is an actual portrait of Soriano and not a stock plate used by printers, as sometimes happened.[16] An oil portrait dated 1590 can also be found in the G. B. Martini Music Library in Bologna.[17]

In the preface to the Mass book, Soriano states that he has held the position of *maestro di cappella* in the three most important churches in the Christian world (Santa Maria Maggiore, St. John Lateran, and St. Peter's), and these works represent some of his labors from those years. Soriano gives no further clue as to exact dates for these compositions, so we must assume that the span of the composition of these Masses falls in the period 1587-1609.

The following year a remarkable publication appears under the title *Canoni et oblighi di 110 sorte, sopra l'Ave maris stella*. This series of canons is for three, four, five, six, seven, and eight voices. The dedication, in Latin, is to Duke Maximilian of Bavaria. In it Soriano speaks of his admiration of the Duke and of his desire to dedicate something suitable to the man who had been the patron of Orlando Lassus and other great musicians, a patron who had done so much to further the arts. With the permission of the Duke's ambassador, Julius Caesar Eribellus, Soriano wished to dedicate this work to the Duke, a work that was an offering to the Mother of God.

In the introduction, in Italian, he modestly admits that his friends had urged him to publish these canons, based on a theme which was considered difficult for canonic treatment. He observes that most people would find the work somewhat dry, but it might serve as a good study for anyone interested in composition.

In 1577 Pope Gregory XIII had commissioned Palestrina and Zoilo to examine the chant books issued after publication of the new *Breviary* and *Missal* ordered by the Council of Trent. They were instructed to cleanse the plain-song of "barbarisms, obscurities, contrarieties, and superfluities as a result of clumsiness or negligence, or even wickedness of composers, scribes, and printers."[18] Even though these two composers set out to complete the assigned task, it remained unfinished at the time of Palestrina's death. His only

16. A similar pose can be seen in Gustave Fellerer's *Palestrina*, p. 48.
17. Paul Kast, "Francesco Soriano."
18. Oliver Strunk, *Source Readings in Music History*, p. 358.

surviving son, Iginio, attempted to have the work completed by others and then offered it to the church as the genuine product. It was rejected, and finally in 1611, Pope Paul V ordered Cardinal del Monte to head a commission and assigned two musicians to finish the task.[19] He picked Francesco Soriano, director of music at St. Peter's, and Felice Anerio, successor to Palestrina as composer to the papal choir. These two men had the task completed within a year; it was submitted to the commission and promptly accepted. There was some delay in the publication, but finally it appeared in 1614 as the *Editio Medicae*. The short period of time needed to revise this considerable body of music leads scholars such as Moliter and Nikel to speculate that the two composers had access to Palestrina's notes and music concerning this work, but there is no conclusive evidence to support this.[20]

Two single compositions of Soriano appear in the next several years, "Credidi" in *Raccolta dei Salmi*, a collection printed in Naples in 1615, and "Ecce sacerdos" in *Selecta cantiones*, a collection by Fabio Gostantini which appeared in 1614. Baini lists two volumes of *Psalmi et Motecta, quae octo, duodecim, et sexdecim voci*, printed by J. Vincentius, the first in 1614 and the second in 1616.[21] There is no indication as to where Baini received his information on the former. It is further recorded by some encyclopedias, but no further mention was found in the library catalogues consulted. Could it be that the 1616 edition, which indeed has *Liber secundus* printed on the title page, is a companion piece to the *Motectorum* of 1597 which lists *Liber primus* on its title page? The *Liber secundus* is printed in thirteen part books, one of which is a *basso continuo* for organ, with figures above the lines. Of the twenty numbers in the collection, fifteen are *a 8*, three *a 12*, and two *a 16*.

Another publication attributed to Soriano by Baini is *Le villanelle a tre voci*, published by Vincenti in Venice in 1617. Haberl doubts that this publication ever existed, not only because there are no extant copies, but the *villanella* had long since gone out of fashion and was not appearing in complete publications at that date. This title is also included in later dictionaries and encyclopedias.

19. Raphael Moliter, *Die nach-tridentinische Choral-Reform zu Rom*, II, 62 ff.

20. Emil Nikel, *Geschichte der katholischen Kirchenmusik*, pp. 310 ff.

21. Baini, *op. cit.*, II, 30.

In 1619 Soriano issued an edition of Guidetti's *Cantus Ecclesiasticus Officii Maioris Hebdomadae* which was published by Andrae Phaei in Rome. From the title page we get another bit of information: "Baselicae S. Mariae Maioris de Urbe Beneficiato Decano, ac Vaticanae Cappellae Praefectio emendatus, et ad meliorem vocum concentus redactus." Thus we are informed that he was a deacon and had a benefice from Santa Maria Maggiore.

The last major publication of Soriano is the *Passio D. N. Jesu Christe secundum quatuor Evangelistas, Magnificat, Sexdedim; Sequentia fidelium Defunctorum, una cum Responsorio,* dated 1619. Included in the work are five Marian antiphons. In the preface, Soriano remarks that part of this book appeared in print fifteen years earlier but does not mention which part. The date of this would then be about 1604, a period that shows little in the way of publication (1603-9). No such publication has been located. The title page of the *Passio* (Plate II) contains a medallion picture with the inscription *Fran. Sur. Rom. An. Ael. Suae LXX*, which sets the year of his birth at 1549. In the center part of the title page appear thirty coats-of-arms of the canons of St. Peter's, to whom the work is dedicated.

A final composition appears in Robblettis' *Lilia campi* of 1624, a four-voice "Ingrediente Domino." Baini gives Soriano's date of death as January, 1620, but this is not likely, for his pension began on May 23 of that year when he was succeeded by Vinc. Agolini of Perugia. Soriano made his will entirely in favor of the Basilica Liberiana with the following provisions: that the capital be used for funeral expenses, that a perpetual Mass in his favor be founded, and that two chaplain offices be established. It is not known for certain when Soriano died, but it was probably after 1621, and he was no doubt buried in Santa Maria Maggiore according to his wishes.

Criticism of the works of Soriano is varied. We have the word of Palestrina that he considered him every bit as good as Marenzio in composition. Sebastian Raval, as reported by Baini, never spoke of Soriano without the title of *signore maestro* after the contest in 1593. In the dedication to a collection of puzzle canons published in 1623, Paolo Masotti notes that many canons appear in the works of Palestrina and others, but Soriano had produced a truly scholarly work in his book of canons on the *Ave maris stella* theme. Another flowery tribute to Soriano's powers as a contrapuntalist is found in

Giovanni d'Avella's book *Regole di musica*, published in Rome in 1667. Adverse criticism is given by Giovanni Doni: "Even though Soriano was very learned in counterpoint, he never had the gift to compose beautiful arias. He instead occupied himself with the composition of canons and other boring vocal works."[22]

Modern criticism has been slightly more detailed, especially after a few examples of Soriano's music found their way into modern editions; but even these are restricted to a sparse sampling consisting mostly of three Masses: *Missa nos autem gloriari*, *Missa super voces musicales*, and *Missa in Papae Marcelli*. These were published by Carl Proske between 1850-9 in his various editions. Sections of the dramatic-type Passions according to Matthew, Mark, Luke, and John appear in several studies in the latter part of the nineteenth century.

Ambros speaks of the first Mass in glowing terms: "Among the masters of the Roman school, Soriano is perhaps the one who shows a powerful energetic craftmanship; in this sense he can be compared to the Netherland school. In his Mass *Nos autem gloriari* the motives seem to be chiseled out of marble in the way they appear so pure, sharp, and firmly defined. The scale-wise motives which race one after the other in the first Kyrie seem to indicate that the Master wished to storm the gates of heaven . . . we can name Soriano along with Anerio (Felice) and Victoria as the Masters who deserve to be favorably compared to Palestrina."[23]

Peter Wagner does not find the *Missa nos autem gloriari* one of the best examples of the Roman school. He calls the style stilted and monotonous and says that it reminds him of the Masses of Clemens non Papa because of the primary concern for contrapuntal correctness. The *Hexachord Mass* is much more to his liking, and he holds it to be one of the best examples of the Roman school composed in the spirit of the *cantus-firmus* type.[24] Pedrell, whom we have already discussed, can be excused for his rather heated criticism on grounds of nationalistic fervor.

A survey of music dictionaries and lexicons gives a diverse picture of Soriano's life and works. Most of the inaccuracies found can be traced back to Baini. The Eitner *Quellen-Lexikon* gives an acceptable biography and list of known publications. The extant

22. Haberl, "Lebensgang und Werke des Francesco Soriano," p. 103.
23. August Wilhelm Ambros, *Geschichte der Musik*, IV, 99, 101.
24. Peter Wagner, *Geschichte der Messe*, p. 431.

manuscripts he mentions are without exception in score and are later copies from the printed works of Soriano.

In the *Dizionario Universale dei Musicisti*, Schmidl includes the first book of *Psalmi* and *Villanelle*. To this he adds one other piece of information, that in 1600 Soriano was *maestro di cappella* at Tivoli Cathedral. This does not fit the suggested chronology of this study, but there is a slight possibility that he could briefly have held that position between the change from St. John Lateran to Santa Maria Maggiore.

Though Grove's *Dictionary of Music and Musicians* gives an acceptable chronology and list of compositions, it somehow has Soriano die at the city of his birth and then be brought to Rome for burial. Moser's *Musik Lexikon* includes the 1614 edition of the *Psalmi*, while the Riemann *Musik Lexikon* does not but does include the *Villanelle* of 1617. Riemann also has some confusion as to dates: Soriano is placed at St. Luigi in 1580-1 and again in 1588. Not until 1583 is he found at Mantua.

In his article "Francesco Soriano" in *Die Musik in Geschichte und Gegenwart*, Paul Kast includes a reproduction of an oil portrait of Soriano which he dates from 1590, now located in the G. B. Martini Music Library in Bologna. This article contains a list of known works, a comprehensive bibliography, and a satisfactory evaluation of Soriano's style.

2. STRUCTURE

In the *Missarum liber primus* Soriano divides his Masses so that there are as few as nine and as many as fifteen sections. The Kyrie normally has the usual three divisons, except for the *Missa ad canones* which is treated as a single unit. Soriano also follows the common practice of dividing the Gloria into two sections, *Et in terra pax* and *Qui tollis*. But again the *Missa ad canones* has no divisions. The Credo sections show from two to four divisions—those most frequently used by Soriano are the *Patrem omnipotentem, Et incarnatus est, Crucifixus, Et resurrexit,* and *Et iterum*. Occasionally *Et in Spiritum* is also used to begin a section. The divisions of the movements are left to the discretion of the composer.

The Sanctus consists of only five sentences, and composers of the late Renaissance usually made three divisions: Sanctus, Hosanna, and Benedictus. When this form was followed, the Hosanna was repeated after the Benedictus, whether the rubric *ut supra* was given or not.

A problem arises in the Agnus Dei where the endings to the three intonations are clearly set forth: *Miserere nobis, miserere nobis,* and *dona nobis pacem*. The priest does not intone this section of the Mass; it is left for the choir to sing or chant. If only one Agnus Dei is composed with the *ut supra* indicated, does this mean that the movement is repeated once with the same words and a third time with the words *dona nobis pacem* inserted? If no rubric at all is given, does the choir sing the polyphonic setting and then finish the rest in plain-chant?

Peter Wagner notes that originally the Agnus Dei was repeated as long as it took to complete the ceremony of the Kiss of Peace, but it was soon reduced to three intonations. The *dona nobis pacem* was universally adopted shortly thereafter with the exception of the Lateran Church in Rome, the church of the Pope. Here they still sing the *miserere nobis* three times. Wagner says that because of the prestige attached to that church, composers often closed their Masses with a single Agnus Dei.[1] To maintain liturgical correctness at other churches, in the opinion of Father Thomas E. Porter, the Agnus Dei I should be repeated with the necessary

1. Wagner, *op. cit.,* p. 9.

12

change in the text to *dona nobis pacem*, an easy transition since both endings have six syllables.[2] In his eight Masses Soriano adds the Agnus Dei II five times.

In the late Renaissance there were five main types of Masses in use:

1. Parody Mass—One which is founded on some pre-existent polyphonic composition which incorporates musical material of the model, both in melody and contrapuntal texture. Sometimes the whole musical fabric is taken over for a few measures, one of the characteristics but not prerequisites of a parody Mass.

2. Tenor Mass, or *Cantus Firmus* Mass—One in which a melody, plainsong, secular song, or some form of traditional tune, is used for the basis for all movements of the Mass. The melody is usually presented in long notes in the tenor but often appears in other voices.

3. Paraphrase Mass—One in which a *cantus firmus* melody, or part of it, is broken up and then ornamented melodically or rhythmically.

4. Canon Mass—One which consists of various types of canon with diverse combination of voices.

5. Free Mass—One which makes no definite use of pre-existent materials. Many of the so-called free Masses which appear as *sine nomine* are, in fact, parody or paraphrase Masses, possibly so titled as to escape ecclesiastical censure.

To these we can add one more for this present discussion, an arrangement of one composer's Mass by another composer for more or less voices, the main outlines including tonality, modality, and length remaining essentially the same.

The procedures employed in composition in the late Renaissance were:

1. Imitative—That which was based more or less strictly on imitation of melodic motives; canonic in extended cases.

2. Homophonic—That in which all voices proceed more or less in identical rhythm.

3. Free—That in which melodic and rhythmic independence is maintained, i.e., without imitation.

The *Missa nos autem gloriari, a 4* is based on six motives found in the Palestrina motet of the same name (Ex. 1a), all of which appear in original or altered form in each major Mass section. Though

2. Interview with Father Thomas E. Porter, S.J. (March 19, 1964).

Ex. 1a. Palestrina, *Nos autem gloriari*.
Ex. 1b. Soriano, *Missa nos autem gloriari*, Kyrie.

there are few instances where a verbatim quotation of the madrigal is given aside from the head motives, there are relatively few measures in the Mass where the borrowed material is not present (Ex. 1b). Only one section is in homophonic style, and the only points of imitation not based on the model are in the Credo and the Agnus Dei II.

The *Missa ad canones, a 4* may be classified as a canon Mass, but other factors place it in the parody class. Since it has canon, however, in every section and sub-section, even in the *Crucifixus* which generally is given separate treatment in Masses of this type in the late Renaissance, it can properly be termed a canon Mass. As to a further classification as a parody Mass, a comparison with the Palestrina Mass, *Missa ad fugam*, brings similarities to light that seem to be more than chance.

The head motive of the Mass sections and their sub-sections provide the first signs of parody. In the Kyrie of Soriano's work, the opening *d-e-d,* answered by *g-a-g,* is the same as that found in Palestrina's Mass, though rhythmically altered. Another motive based on an ascending tetrachord, used by both composers in various subsections, can be definitely related. Other sections of both works, such as in the Gloria, at the text *Qui tollis peccata mundi,* have not only the same rhythm and general contours but also identical text underlay.

The most striking parody comes at the *Amen* of the Credo (Ex. 2). Palestrina's characteristic figure here is a dotted minim, followed by three semiminims in descending motion, passing several times through each voice. Soriano alters the rhythm which now becomes dotted minim-semiminim-minim. This figure is used to such an extent that a sequence is formed over five measures, something Palestrina avoids.

Soriano departs from Palestrina's model in the Agnus Dei I and II. He retains the pair of canons with resolution at the upper fourth, but adds to each a hymn melody with text, set in semibreves as a *cantus firmus.* These hymns are *Ave maris stella*[3] and *Iste confessor.*[4] Just why Soriano used two hymns with no apparent connection in this Mass is not clear; perhaps it was intended for the celebration of a feast day no longer observed. One small clue

---

3. *Liber Usualis,* p. 1259.
4. Constantius Festa, *Hymni per Totum Annum,* p. 155. This is the closest variant found.

15

was found: a letter illumination in the Sanctus at the Benedictus contains the text incipit *Beatam me dicent,* an antiphon used before the Magnificat and following the *Ave maris stella* during second Vespers on the second of July. This is the feast of *The Visitation of the Blessed Virgin Mary,* but no similarities were noted be-

Ex. 2a. Palestrina, *Missa ad fugam*, Credo, 116.
Ex. 2b. Soriano, *Missa ad canones*, Credo, 126.

tween this antiphon and the Benedictus of the *Missa ad canones.* Soriano's connection with the Santa Maria Maggiore Basilica through the years 1587-99 and 1601-3 no doubt afforded him ample occasions to supply compositions based on this topic.

The *Missa sine titulo* is a five-voice Mass in the Aeolian mode, and though it appears as one without a title, it has been identified as a parody of the famous Palestrina madrigal *Vestiva i colli,* which first appeared in print in 1566. Not only was this madrigal frequently reprinted, but it became the object of widespread parody treatment, both sacred and secular. Hans Moser notes that parody Masses on this madrigal were composed by Palestrina himself, G. M. Nanini, Giovanelli, Belli, Cesena, Nucius, and Rudolf Lassus.[5] To this list Gustave Reese adds a Mass by Monte and a parody by Banchieri in the madrigal comedy *La Pazzia senile* of 1598.[6] Soriano makes extensive use of both sections of the madrigal and presents the borrowed material not only in its natural state but also in augmentation and diminution.

The *Missa Quando laeta sperabam, a 5* is based on Cipriano de Rore's madrigal *Quando lieta sperai* with the sonnet text by Emilia Anguisciola. Bernhard Meier notes that this was also a popular subject for parody; examples include Masses by Andrea Gabrieli and Phillipe de Monte, a Magnificat by Lassus, and a lute *intavolature* published in a collection by Vincenzo Galilei.[7] To this we can add a parody Mass by Palestrina and another by Soriano.

The Masses by Palestrina and Soriano have only the model in common, for while Palestrina chooses a few themes from the madrigal for development, Soriano uses themes from practically every musical idea of Rore's work, which is in itself through-composed. Soriano's stylized treatment of this material, plus his own additions and alterations, seems to follow a broad plan. The opening paired-imitation of the model is used as a head motive by Soriano to begin the Kyrie I, Credo, Sanctus, Hosanna, and Agnus Dei II. This gives a sense of unity and a structural outline at the highest level, but an even more detailed attempt at formal groupings by the head motive can be seen in the Sanctus.

After its initial presentation in the Sanctus, the head motive appears with new accompanying counterpoint in the first Hosanna, which is literally repeated in the second Hosanna, first at meas. 74-78 and again at the section beginning at meas. 85-93. The resultant form is roughly ABA¹CA¹. Other sections show some traces of ABA form but none as clearly stated as in the Hosanna. Other sections in this Mass use a through-composed technique by introducing successive points of imitation. Soriano also emphasizes

5. Hans Moser, "Vestiva i colli," pp. 129 ff.
6. Reese, *op. cit.,* p. 403.
7. Cipriani Rore, *Opera Omnia,* p. 11.

17

structural outlines of the Mass in the traditional manner by changing the texture in some of the sub-sections, either by reducing the
number of parts or employing a combination of voices in a higher
register. Except for the recurring head motive, the use of the
melodic material from the model indicates a free form of parody,
especially since there is no section where there is a simultaneous

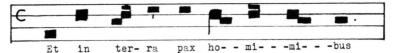

Et   in   ter- ra   pax   ho- - mi- - -mi- - -bus

Et in terra pax ho-mi-ni-bus bonae voluntatis. Laudau - mus te.

Ex. 3a. *Liber Usualis*, Gloria, p. 86.
Ex. 3b. *Missa octavi toni*, Gloria, 1.

appearance of all voices of the model, a characteristic though not
indispensable mark of a parody.

The *Missa octavi toni, a* 5 has all of the appearances of being a
combination of a tenor Mass and a paraphrase Mass. There is one
problem in classifying it, the lack of a model from which it is
drawn. Only at two points can any connection be made with a

Qui   tol- lis   pec- ca- - - ta   mun- - - di

Qui   tol- lis   pec- - ca- - - - - ta_____ mun-di.

Ex. 4a. *Liber Usualis*, p. 87.
Ex. 4b. *Missa octavi toni*, Gloria, 50.

known plain-chant melody, and then only for a very few measures.
The first is in the cantus of the Gloria, meas. 1-10, which corresponds to an eleventh-century Gloria found in the *Liber Usualis*,
page 86 (Ex. 3). The second is also in the Gloria (meas. 50) and
in the same chant of the *Liber Usualis* beginning at the *Qui tollis*
(Ex. 4). No other quotation or paraphrase of this particular chant

could be connected with Soriano's Mass, a fact that somewhat weakens the paraphrase theory.

A factor pointing to a tenor Mass is that every Mass-movement has a *cantus firmus*, sometimes restricted to one voice, sometimes divided among voices. It appears in various rhythmic variations, sometimes even in breves, as in the Kyrie II, where the archaic practice of *canon cancrizans* is demonstrated, with canon in the tenor and resolution in the cantus. There are few recurring motives to give structural outline to the work as a whole; rather, the *cantus firmus* material, whatever that may be, is closely woven with a contrapuntal texture based on presumably freely constructed points of imitation.

The *Missa secundi toni, a 6* is a transposed Dorian with its final on g with one flat as its key signature. There is no identifiable use of *cantus firmus* or paraphrase of Gregorian melody, which one normally expects from Masses with such titles. Examination of the Mass shows that nine of the thirteen sections use a head motive, presented each time in essentially the same harmonic pattern. This progression corresponds to the first five measures of the *passamezzo moderno*, one of the five basic isometric bass patterns, which made its appearance around 1540 and was published as such in D. Ortiz' *Trato de glosas* of 1553 (Ex. 5).

Reese mentions that "the middle of the century marks the disappearance of the *pavana* in favor of its less solemn equivalent, the *passamezzo antico* or the *passamezzo moderno* (or *comune*)."[8] Manfred Bukofzer, writing about the early Baroque practice of using such melodies, states, "Certain traditional bass melodies, some of which went back to Renaissance music, served as the basis for vocal and instrumental variations or furnished the harmonic foundation for the improvised singing of popular poetry (*ottave rime*) . . . the basses were only skeletal melodies each note of which appeared on the first beat of every measure, thus guiding the succession of harmonies."[9]

Soriano does not use the progression as a basis for improvisation, but one observation made from all sources consulted concerning *passamezzi* is that the practice seems to have been confined to secular works. If this head motive can be accepted as a partial quotation of the *passamezzo moderno*, it is the only instance known to

8. Reese, *op. cit.*, p. 524.
9. Manfred Bukofzer, *Music in the Baroque Era*, p. 40.

the author where this bass was incorporated into a Mass. Except for the beginnings of sections, the head motive appears only three times, and apart from these quotations is not developed further in the various Mass-movements.

It could well be that Soriano was simply making a nod to one of the popular forms of the day, and since Frescobaldi was organ-

Ex. 5a. Soriano, VI Kyrie, 1.
Ex. 5b. *Passamezzo moderno* after John Ward in *M.G.G.*

ist at St. Peter's Basilica prior to the publication of this Mass, it is conceivable that Soriano was well informed as to the very latest techniques for instrumental and vocal forms. In his book, *Tonality and Atonality in Sixteenth-Century Music,* Edward Lowinsky notes: "The *passamezzo antico* bass affording a harmonic progression close to modern minor had its counterpart in the *passamezzo moderno* yielding harmonic progressions in a clear tonal major, whereas the related *Zefiro* is a hybrid between a tonal and modal cadence. It is tempting to interpret the term *passamezzo moderno* as indicating awareness on the part of the sixteenth-century musician that the 'tonal' pattern of the *passamezzo moderno* constitutes something novel."[10] It is likewise tempting for the author to interpret Soriano's treatment of the *passamezzo moderno* as a rejection of the major in favor of a mixed modality, showing his preference for the *stile antico*.

As in the *Missa super voces musicales,* the six tones of the hexachord have been repeatedly used as a *cantus firmus* for vocal or instrumental compositions. Vocal compositions are found in the works of A. Gabrieli, P. Vinci, Jacob de Kerle, A. Bota, Tresti, Artusini, Palestrina, and Soriano.[11] Instrumental pieces, mostly keyboard fantasies and ricercari, also appear in the works of Giuliano Tiburtino, Sweelinck, Bull, Byrd, Farrabosco, Hassler, Scheidt, Frescobaldi, Froberger, and Albrechtsberger.[12]

Of the two predecessors of Soriano who served as *maestro di cappella* at Santa Maria Maggiore, Palestrina and Vinci supply possible models to which Soriano probably had access. Vinci's Mass can be eliminated after the most superficial examination. However, when comparing Palestrina's *Missa Ut, Re, Mi, Fa, Sol, La* with the Soriano Mass, the differences as well as the similarities seem to indicate that Soriano was not only familiar with Palestrina's Mass, but was attempting to explore further the possibilities of a composition based on the hexachord, perhaps to demonstrate his own technical skill.

The divisions of the two Masses are alike except in the Sanctus. Here Palestrina had a separate CCAA setting for the *Pleni sunt coeli* terminating at the Hosanna, while Soriano treats the Sanctus as a single unit. Both composers use a four-voice setting for the *Crucifixus* and *Benedictus*. We may note that, as we make a line-by-line comparison of the two works, at many places where Palestrina begins in imitation, Soriano begins in more homophonic fashion. The reverse is also true to the extent that it looks as though Soriano were trying to avoid any parody of the Palestrina Mass. Aside from motives arising from imitation of the hexachord, there are no the-

10. Edward Lowinsky, *Tonality and Atonality in Sixteenth-Century Music,* p. 68.
11. Gustav Fellerer, *Palestrina,* p. 91.
12. Martin Ruhnke, "Hexachord," col. 357.

21

matic similarities in the two works. The Palestrina Mass is also 125 measures longer than Soriano's, most of the difference coming as a result of longer sub-sections in the Sanctus and Agnus Dei I and II.

Palestrina always has the *cantus firmus* in the cantus II with a single exception in the Agnus Dei II, where the *resolutio* of a canon comes at the lower fifth. The cantus II uses the *hexachordum durum*, ascending and descending, and this hexachord appears at other times in the other voices as well as the *hexachordum naturale*, but the *hexachordum molle* is never present.

Soriano alternates the *cantus firmus* mainly between the cantus I and cantus II. The exceptions to this are found in the Kyrie I and Sanctus, where it appears several times in the tenor (Ex. 6). In the four-voice Benedictus, the *cantus firmus* appears in the cantus three times and two times each in the other voices. Palestrina's Agnus Dei II *a 7* has a canon with *resolutio* at the lower fifth; Soriano sets his Agnus II for eight voices with a mirror canon based on the hard hexachord, the canon in the tenor II with *resolutio* in the cantus II.

The rhythmic pattern of the *cantus firmus* is regular in the Palestrina Mass; that is to say, he moves the melody up and down in strict half-measure, measure, or more. His only departure from this procedure is in the Gloria and *Crucifixus*. Soriano allows himself much greater freedom in his rhythmic treatment of the *cantus firmus* and has much more of a mixture of note values, ascending and descending.

Soriano, in the Mass book of 1609, was the first to publish an arrangement of the *Marcellus Mass* of Palestrina. A Mantuan composer named Stefano Nascimbini reputedly included a twelve-voice arrangement of Palestrina's Mass in a collection titled *Concerti ecclesiastici* for three choirs, published in 1610. G. F. Nanino published his four-part arrangement of the *Marcellus Mass* in 1619, and in 1850 Carl Proske published the Masses of Palestrina, Soriano, and Nanino in score under the title *Missa Papae Marcelli triplici*.

In order to expand Palestrina's Mass to double chorus, Soriano adds a cantus and altus. The only departures from the general plan as set down by Palestrina are in the Sanctus and Benedictus; here Soriano uses borrowed thematic material from the model with different voice combinations. In the rest of the Mass, Soriano is more consistent in following the outlines of the model. This is a

Ex. 6. VII Kyrie, 1.

creative process insofar as he is adding material to the original and not reducing it for fewer voice parts or solo instrument. The two bassus parts are most nearly like those of the model, and these form the basis of the harmony. The cantus of the model is sometimes divided between the cantus parts in Soriano's arrangement. The added cantus material is sometimes in counterpoint; often it moves in parallel thirds. The inner parts of the two choruses tend to be more free rather than simply following the model. Sometimes, as in the *Patrem* section of the Credo, the whole texture is translated into double chorus, especially where Palestrina has four voice-groups alternating much like a double chorus.

However, Palestrina is not concerned with double chorus but rather with a six-voice complex from which he draws various timbres through the manipulation of voice-groups. For example, in the first twenty-two measures of the Credo, there are six different voice-groupings, while Soriano restricts himself to alternation of groups and both groups together. Some melodic and rhythmic changes are made, but only one cadential change is made, that in the Gloria where the close at meas. 54 is changed from V-I to IV-I.

One curious change occurs in Soriano's treatment of the *nota cambiata*. Of the twenty-two counted in the model, Soriano avoids twelve of them by changing the melodic line, but nonetheless, eleven were counted in the arrangement. Of these eleven, six were turned into cambiatas, because he added a fourth voice to accommodate the double chorus. Throughout the compositions of Soriano examined by the author, this seems to be a characteristic—he simply avoids the cambiata figure. Degree inflection and use of accidentals are frequent enough to indicate a certain modern outlook.

3. MELODY

The basis of the polyphony of the Masses of Soriano, like that of Palestrina, is melody. In an analysis of the works under consideration, it was expected that the general rules as compiled from the music of Palestrina by Jeppesen would be valid for the Masses of Soriano. With a few important exceptions this was indeed the case. This chapter follows the two Jeppesen studies for melodic analysis, and the differences as well as similarities noted should help determine the style of Soriano.[1]

A typical Palestrina curvilinear form could best be described as one in which ascending and descending movements counterbalance each other with almost mathematical accuracy. The first example from the Masses of Soriano shows a short theme with the ambitus of a sixth (Ex. 1). Most of the movement is by step; but

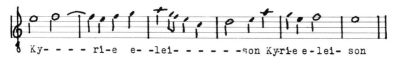

Ky- - - - ri-e e- -lei- - - - - -son Kyrie e-lei- son

Ex. 1. IV Kyrie, 3.

the rise and fall of the melodic line is well balanced, and the two climax points do not favor either the beginning or the end of the phrase.

Example 2 shows a more active melody with a much wider

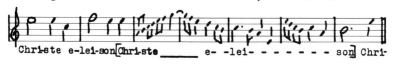

Christe e-lei-son Christe _____ e- -lei- - - - - - son Chri-

Ex. 2. IV Kyrie, 29.

range, but it also has the same sense of balance and proportion. This melody contains most of the intervals normally used in the Palestrina style: major and minor seconds, major and minor thirds, perfect fourth, perfect fifth, and perfect octave. The ascending skip of a minor sixth is also permitted.

Descending minor sixth, major sixth, augmented or diminished intervals, and intervals greater than an octave do not occur in the Masses of Soriano. Occasionally these intervals will be found

1. Knud Jeppesen, *Counterpoint* and *The Style of Palestrina and the Dissonance, passim.*

Ex. 3a. VII Gloria, 52.
Ex. 3c. VII Credo, 50.

Ex. 3b. VII Credo, 42.
Ex. 3d. VII Credo, 64.

Ex. 3e. VII Credo, 139.   Ex. 3f. VIII Gloria, 1.

between the final note in one melodic phrase and the initial tone of the next, the so-called "dead" interval.

One departure from the Palestrina style by Soriano is his use of chromatic half-steps, that is, the half-step which arises from the progression of a tone to its chromatic alteration, as C to C-sharp or B to B-flat. To distinguish this from accidentals which do not give rise to semitonal progression, Reese names the former "degree inflection,"[2] a term which will be used in this connection in this study. The examples of degree inflection noted in Ex. 3 are confined to Masses VII and VIII and do not constitute a general shift away from the Palestrina style, but it is an expressive device also used by other composers of the late Renaissance.[3]

A survey of the secular and sacred works of Soriano composed both before and after the Mass book shows few additional instances of degree inflection. Example 3f is the remarkable quotation from the *Missa in Papae Marcelli*, where one would not ordinarily expect to find an infraction of this rule. As noted in the chapter on structure, Soriano takes more liberties in the application of accidentals than did Palestrina.

This would seem to be an appropriate place to discuss another departure from the Palestrina style, the melodic sequence. Again, there is no great profusion of infractions of the general rule which excludes sequences. Those that appear in the Masses of Soriano, however, are such that they cannot be considered accidental. The

2. Reese, *op. cit.*, p. 16.
3. *Ibid.*, p. 484.

27

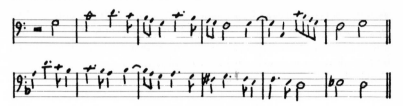

Ex. 4a. Palestrina, *Missa ad fugam*, Credo, 116.
Ex. 4b. Soriano, II, Credo, 127.

first of these has been quoted in its entirety in Ex. 1 of Chapter II. This *Amen* passage from the Credo of the *Missa ad canones* is a parody of the Palestrina counterpart, and a further examination of the two bassus lines at this point would be helpful (Ex. 4).

Technically speaking, the repetition of the figure in Ex. 4a is a melodic sequence, and Jeppesen notes that "in general, Palestrina uses them only rarely (mostly in earlier works), since balance of the linear treatment can easily be displaced by the overemphasis which they place upon a particular motive."[4] The work in question comes from Palestrina's second book of Masses, published

Ex. 5. VII Credo, 184.

4. Jeppesen, *Counterpoint*, p. 84.

28

in 1567. Soriano breaks this melodic figure into a three-note motive and repeats it five times in a descending progression. The sequence figure is not confined to the bassus but appears in the tenor (seven times), altus (four times), and cantus (four times).

Another pair of examples appear in the *Missa super voces musicales,* just a few measures apart. The first one (Ex. 5) shows sequence patterns in three of the six voices, the bassus, tenor I, and cantus II. The bassus descends by step on the first beat of

Ex. 6.   VII Credo, 194.

meas. 185-89 and parallels the *cantus firmus* at the interval of a fifth on the first beat of each measure. This parallel movement is obscured by the upward movement of the bassus on the second and third beats. The cantus II and tenor also offset the feeling of parallel movement by an overlapping ascending semiminim passage in sequence, which fills in the third of the interval established by the outer voices.

Example 6 shows the *cantus firmus* ascending in breve movement accompanied at the lower octave on the first beat of each measure by the bassus. Again the bassus has an ascending movement on the other beats of the measure. No melodic sequence is found in the other voices which engage in free counterpoint, and the two tenor voices at times dip below the bassus and supply the harmonic outline which is non-sequential.

In the Palestrina style, a melodic movement should be such that it not call undue attention to itself; when a skip takes place, there are certain compensating movements introduced which tend to give balance to the phrase. This is especially true in semiminim movement, where the general rules are more closely observed.

Normally, skips in semiminim movement are compensated for by stepwise movement or skips in the other direction. Example 7a

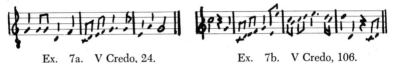

Ex. 7a. V Credo, 24.   Ex. 7b. V Credo, 106.

shows a skip down a fourth which is compensated for by a skip up a third; another skip downward of a fourth is then answered by stepwise movement in semiminims in the opposite direction. Example 7b shows a more extreme case: the skip down of a fifth is answered by ascending stepwise movement back to the note of departure. Then a descending skip of a third is followed by an octave leap which in turn falls back a third. After moving down a step, it climbs up to the climax note where it pauses before an ornamental turn and finally drops an octave.

Often it happens that a skip will follow another skip in the same direction, or skips and stepwise progression alternate. Jeppesen gives two rules which cover most of these situations:[5]

1. In ascending movement it is better to have the larger intervals at the beginning of the curve; the larger skip should therefore precede the smaller (Ex. 8a).

Ex. 8a. V Credo, 200.   Ex. 8b. V Gloria, 77.

2. In descending motion, on the other hand, the smaller intervals generally precede the larger (Ex. 8b).

In values larger than a semiminim, these rules are regarded as tendencies which are usually observed but can be overlooked for

5. *Ibid.*, p. 86.

more important considerations. Also, skips in series which take place over a "dead" interval are given freer treatment, as in Ex. 9a where a skip of a fifth follows a skip of a fourth in ascending motion. Even the forbidden interval of the major sixth can be admitted under the same circumstances (Ex. 9b).

Ex. 9a. V Credo, 57.   Ex. 9b. VIII Credo, 57.

More than two skips in the same direction are generally avoided, especially in semiminim movement. No such examples were found in the Masses of Soriano, but in larger note-values they occasionally occur.

Jeppesen formulates one rule concerning the treatment of ascending skips from accented portions of the measure which he names the "high-note law." This is *an avoidance as far as possible of ascending leaps from accentuated to unaccented crotchets* [semiminims]."[6] Larger note-values are not strictly regulated by this law (Ex. 10a), but the tendency remains for ascending skips to occur on the unaccented portion of the measure (Ex. 10b).

Ex. 10a.   V Kyrie, 31.   Ex. 10b.   V Gloria, 68.

When it comes to note-values smaller than the minim, the "high-note law" is strictly observed in the Masses of Soriano. No exception was found.

In descending semiminim skips from the accented beats, about thirty-seven per cent of those counted were found in the arrangement of the *Marcellus Mass*. In matching different types with the thirty-five melodic ornamentation-types shown by Jeppesen,[7] only about half appear in the Masses of Soriano. The strongest tendency is for the semiminims to continue in conjunct motion, and when a skip occurs, more often than not it comes on an unaccented beat.

Semiminim auxiliary notes are found frequently in the works of Soriano. One hundred and twenty-three were counted in the first four Masses. Of these, only three are upper dissonant returning

6. Jeppesen, *The Style of Palestrina and the Dissonance*, p. 65.
7. *Ibid.*, pp. 61-62.

notes, and each occurrence is followed by a larger note value. The majority are lower auxiliary notes which appear on the unaccented portion of the measure.

At the fusa level, Jeppesen notes that these were normally used only in groups of two in the sixteenth century and were introduced and quitted in stepwise movement. In the Masses of Soriano, the picture is somewhat different. Though the majority of instances noted follow the general rule, there are frequent places where he departs from what could be considered the Palestrina style. First of all, a comparison of the *Missa Papae Marcelli* of Palestrina and the *Missa in Papae Marcelli* by Soriano shows the latter using about nine times as many fusas in groups of two on the unaccented por-

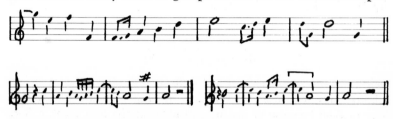

Ex. 11a.   VIII Kyrie, 61.
Ex. 11b.   Palestrina, *Missa Papae Marcelli*, Gloria, 61.
Ex. 11c.   Soriano, VIII Gloria, 95.

tion of the beat. The reason for the significant increase here is probably the necessity of adding melodic and rhythmic interest to a Mass which is rather austere to begin with, and to which Soriano added two parts before dividing it for double chorus. Passing notes and returning notes account for the majority of these additions, but the inclusion of twenty-three figures, consisting of a dotted semiminim followed by a fusa, is entirely new to this Mass (Ex. 11a). In the Gloria at meas. 96, Palestrina abruptly introduces a series of four fusas on the third beat of the measure, the only occurrence in the Mass (Ex. 11b). Soriano alters this to a dotted semiminim and a fusa (Ex. 11c).

Another comparison between Palestrina's *Missa ad fugam* and Soriano's *Missa ad canones* shows Soriano using more fusa pairs than Palestrina, this time twice as many. Palestrina confines himself to the lower returning auxiliary figure, and though Soriano also uses this in a majority of instances, he frequently uses passing notes and dotted patterns, one showing two in a series (Ex. 12a). In the Credo at meas. 70, Soriano gives a syllable of text to a fusa (Ex.

12b), a procedure which is also considered outside of the Palestrina style.

The rule that fusas normally quit the movement by step is not observed in the Masses of Soriano. There are skips up from fusa

Ex. 12a. II Sanctus, 20.
Ex. 12b. II Credo, 70.

pairs to intervals of a third, a fourth, a fifth, and an octave (Ex. 13a-d). Only one fusa was found as an upper neighbor (Ex. 13e). The marked increase of ornamental notes at the fusa level in Soriano's Masses suggests a higher level of activity in the polyphonic complex. To test this premise, the first 135 measures of three Credo movements of Masses of both composers were examined.[8] The re-

Ex. 13a. I Credo, 197.   Ex. 13b. III Sanctus, 87.
Ex. 13c. VIII Credo, 147.   Ex. 13d. IV Sanctus, 18.   Ex. 13e. VI Gloria, 46.

sults show twenty-six per cent more activity at the semiminim level and below in the works of Soriano. This increased activity does not suggest a slower tempo to the author but simply a tendency for Soriano to use more ornamentation.

In a discussion of melody which conforms to the Palestrina ideal, there are also other melody types considered within the style. The first of these is the type with an under-climax with the melody de-

8. Palestrina, *Missa ad fugam, Missa Quando lieta sperai, Missa octavi toni;* Soriano Masses II, IV, and V.

scending almost in mirror motion to the classical curve (Ex. 14). Another type also found frequently in the Palestrina style is the one which is particularly characteristic of Gregorian melodies. This begins at a high level and gradually winds downward, usually

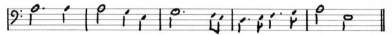

Ex. 14.   IV Sanctus, 46.

through an octave. Sometimes it pauses, turns upwards, and then slips back, but the motion is serene and calm (Ex. 15). One final characteristic of many of these melody types is for the theme to begin in large note-values and end the same way, with the activity increasing in the center portion (Ex. 1 and 2).

Ex. 15.   IV Gloria, 71.

4. POLYPHONY

I n the Masses under consideration we find that Soriano used just about every technique available in the polyphonic style of the period. Depending on the given material and the general plan which he has set for himself, he does not favor one style over another. He uses single subjects, two subjects, fugal imitation around a *cantus firmus*, canon and homophonic style, extensive exploitation of voice-grouping and invertible counterpoint. There are also many sections that could be considered in free style, but Soriano usually includes fragments of familiar thematic material which give a sense of unity and continuity to the whole.

SINGLE-SUBJECT IMITATION

This type is frequent in Soriano's Masses and can be described as a melodic phrase of moderate length with a well-defined character of melody or rhythm or both. Usually, it begins on the final or fifth degree of the scale. Imitations of this melody most often begin at the fifth, octave, unison, or less often at the fourth.

The first example demonstrates a strict treatment of the single-subject imitation (Ex. 1). In this Kyrie I, only one subject is used, and the voices answer in stretto, i.e., before the five measure subject is completed. In meas. 2 the altus answers at the lower fifth, and at meas. 6 the tenor is answered at the lower fifth by the bassus. Between points of imitation the voices engage in free imitation or use fragments of the theme. This can be observed in the tenor voice at meas. 12 where the descending skip of a fourth in semiminims has been used, and two measures later the ascending semiminim figure is repeated in the altus.

While such strict treatment is not encountered all of the time, the following is a style which occurs more frequently in the Masses of Soriano (Ex. 2). The theme is a variant of the head motive and is presented in two forms: a skip up of a third (cantus) and a skip up of a fifth (bassus). In addition, the bassus is paired with the altus at three minims distance from the cantus. The head motive is by now reduced to two measures in length, but it is still unmistakable in its relationship to the original. The tenor entrance in the third measure of this example is the last appearance of the head motive before a section in homophonic style begins. At this point, the composer could also begin a new point of imitation, begin a new point in stretto, or engage in free counterpoint if he so choses. Such examples are common and need no further comment.

Two-Subject Imitation

This type of imitation is fairly common in the Masses of Soriano. It could be described as an imitation in which two subjects are

Ex. 1.   I Kyrie, 1.

announced close together or even as a pair. Sometimes the second subject is delayed until the first has been imitated. The subjects themselves can be similar in melodic and rhythmic design, or they can contrast radically. In the course of a Mass-movement, different

36

treatments including single subjects, homophonic passages, or mix-
tures of all types can take place.

Contrasting subjects are prevalent in these Masses. The next
example (Ex. 3) shows paired subjects at the octave, where theme
A is followed at the distance of a minim by a second theme (B)
which has larger note-values. This second theme has an ambitus of
a fourth and shows more of the classical lines of a Palestrina melody
in that it has graceful curves, balance, and proportion, even though
only about three measures long. Theme A shows almost an im-
mediate semiminim movement to a climax note before it falls back.
Though a little shorter than its contrasting theme, it exhibits great-

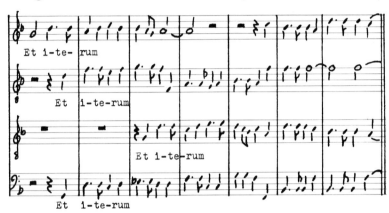

Ex. 2. I Credo, 141.

er rhythmic interest, and this is the one that Soriano develops. The
first note is altered to make a group of ascending semiminims (A¹),
or inversion of the theme (A²). In the fourteen measures of the
example, theme A is presented twelve times as compared with five
entrances of theme B.

An example of a two-subject imitation with similar themes can
be seen in the next example (Ex. 4). This is a canon for the cantus
and tenor with resolution at the lower fifth for the altus and bassus,
at the time interval of a breve. Theme A is imitated in the tenor at
the octave and extended one semibreve. Theme B enters in stretto
in the cantus (meas. 46), and the tenor gives an altered version of
the first theme (A²). This in turn is stated by the cantus in meas.
50 (A³), with the addition of the semiminim figure from the second
half of theme B. The tenor at this point gives an altered version of

37

B. With the addition of the two *resolutio* parts, the effect of thematic exchange among parts is strengthened, and the whole section shows a close-knit polyphonic complex.

FUGAL IMITATION USED IN CONJUNCTION WITH A CANTUS FIRMUS

This archaic style is used frequently in Soriano's Masses: in the *Missa nos autem gloriari*, the Agnus Dei II has a *cantus firmus* in the tenor voice; the *Missa ad canones* has a *cantus firmus* in both

Ex. 3. IV Kyrie, 52.

Agnus Dei I and II, each including the hymn text with which it is associated instead of the Ordinary text; the *Missa octavi toni* seems to be based on plain-chant, and though the *cantus firmus* is unknown in its entirety, traces of chant-like melodies are found in most movements; the *Missa super voces musicales* uses the hexachord ascending and descending in every section and sub-section.

Ex. 4.   II Sanctus, 43.

The use of *cantus firmus* with hymn text or other sacred text in the Ordinary of the Mass dates back to the Middle Ages, but the attitude of church authorities in the late Renaissance discouraged such additions, as they tended to obscure the words. Example 5 is taken from the Agnus Dei II of the *Missa ad canones* and shows the *cantus firmus* in the cantus with the chant melody and the text of the *Ave maris stella*. The bassus has a canon with the reso-

39

Ex. 5. II Agnus Dei, 29.

lution in the tenor at the upper fourth. The altus I and altus II are paired subjects, and these two voices are both complementary to and independent of the *cantus firmus* and canon.

Another type of *cantus firmus* is the kind in which the melody is passed around from voice to voice, while fugal entries on independent subjects are given to the other voices and are subsequently

40

Ex. 6. V Kyrie, 21.

taken up by the part which had been singing the *cantus firmus.*
This technique can be seen in Ex. 6, where what appears to be part
a plain-chant in the cantus is repeated in the tenor II at meas. 3,
the bassus at meas. 8, tenor at meas. 11, and altus I at meas. 13.
In one respect, this resembles a two-subject imitation, but throughout this Mass the same treatment of different melodic fragments in

41

semibreves or breves appears. A *cantus firmus* presented in such a manner is sometimes called a "migrant" *cantus firmus.*[1]

HOMOPHONIC TREATMENT AND VOICE-GROUPINGS

In the Masses there are no extended passages where the voices move in block chords over the same text for more than a few measures. The usual treatment may be observed in Ex. 7: when the text *Jesu Christe* is reached, the voices proceed in breve and semibreve movement for two measures. Upon repetition of the text, however, the homophonic structure dissolves as a new point of imitation is introduced.

Ex. 7.   I Gloria, 94.

More usual is the treatment afforded the *Et incarnatus est* from the *Missa super voces musicales* (Ex. 8). Four of the six voices move in the same rhythm over the same text, but we note that the two tenor parts have melodies which are much more active, though the text points are generally the same. One other point to be noted is Soriano's reluctance to begin any section or sub-section with all voices entering together. One or more voices are generally held back at least a semiminim, a practice also common to the Masses of Palestrina.

Voice-grouping plays a significant role in the Masses with five or more voices. As noted above, Soriano seems to prefer to have some parts moving in sections where it tends to become homophonic. Also it is observed that he prefers higher voice-groupings in the

1. H. K. Andrews, *An Introduction to the Style of Palestrina*, p. 155.

Ex. 8. VII Credo, 64.

Ex. 9. VI Credo, 149.

Ex. 10a.   Palestrina, *Missa Papae Marcelli*, Credo, 25.

sections using a smaller number of parts. It should be emphasized that generally a wide variety of textures is used.

One method of grouping voices can be seen in Ex. 9. A voice-group (CATT) concludes a section at meas. 151, and another group takes over (CATB) until there is a cadence on *g* at meas. 154. Here

Ex. 10b. Soriano, VIII Credo, 25.

the head motive is briefly quoted by the complete choir, and the complex dissolves into imitation of another theme.

The arrangement of the *Marcellus Mass* shows a combination of homophonic treatment and voice-grouping. Along with this, Soriano has the problem of adding more parts to complete the arrangement for double chorus. This he solves in various ways. In Ex. 10a, the Palestrina original shows a CATB passage (meas. 25-27), and a similar group follows with a change in tenor and bassus (meas. 28-

46

29); another section composed of ATTB follows (meas. 30-32) and so forth throughout the example. Except for the overlap of parts, Palestrina has three or four voices sounding except at meas. 35-38.

Usually when there are five voices continuing for any considerable length, Soriano simply composes three new parts; however, in

Ex. 10b (*concluded*). VIII Credo.

this case he omits the tenor II. Aside from slight rhythmic alterations in the cantus and bassus, the parts are taken over as they stand (Ex. 10b). The first exchange of groups (meas. 28) presents no problem as the same four-part groups are present. However, at meas. 30 a cantus must be included in the Chorus I, and Soriano solves this by retaining the altus, tenor II, and bassus as they appear in the original and transposing the tenor I up an octave where it serves as the cantus. At meas. 34, there is no altus part, so one is composed, the usual procedure when one is missing or when a part cannot be transposed or arranged from another part.

Where the model has all six voices singing (Ex. 11a), it means that Soriano must add two parts, a cantus and an altus. Example 11b shows the approach to and departure from such a passage: Soriano uses the cantus, altus, tenor I and bassus II of the model for his Chorus I. For the Chorus II, the bassus I is retained with a few rhythmic alterations; the tenor II is divided between the altus and tenor of Chorus II; the cantus doubles the first part of the tenor I at the octave with the exception of a downward skip of a

Ex. 11a.   Palestrina, *Missa Papae Marcelli*, Credo, 43.

third, whereby parallel octaves are avoided. Other chord notes from the harmony of the passage are used by the cantus to finish out the passage.

Two other Masses have sections with canon: the *Missa octavi toni* has a canon *cancrizans* in the Kyrie II, and the *Missa super voces musicales* has a mirror canon *a 8* with canon in the tenor I and *resolutio* in the cantus II. The *resolutio* is not provided for the *Missa ad canones*.

INVERTIBLE COUNTERPOINT

Invertible counterpoint is also encountered in the Masses, but its use is not exploited simply for the sake of a display of technical virtuosity. Rather it seems to grow naturally out of the imitative procedures employed by the composer. The technique can best be explained as a passage in contrapuntal texture so designed that by

Ex. 11b.   Soriano, VIII Credo, 43.

means of transposition, usually of an octave, the lower part may become the higher part or the higher part the lower. Example 12a shows how the lower voice, when transposed up an octave to the unison with the top voice, becomes the upper part.

Perhaps Soriano's attitude toward such devices can best be observed in Ex. 12b. The transposition of theme A is down a fourth and

Ex. 12a.   I Gloria, 43.

Ex. 12b.   VIII Sanctus, 53.

theme B up a fifth which brings it to an octave relationship. After the first measure of the imitation, the voice-leading in the semi-minim movement is altered in both parts, since there is an approach to a cadence on *g* and not on *d* as before. If the two voices are realized exactly as before at the new pitch level, they do work out in double or invertible counterpoint, but it appears that other considerations were more important, so the alteration is made.

Musical rhyme is not usually found in the Masses. However, there are some instances of melodic cadential formulae which, when repeated often enough, would probably be easily enough discerned by the listener. For example, in the final cadences of seven of the fourteen sections of the *Missa nos autem gloriari*, the same melodic formula is present in the cantus. Of these seven, only two cadences are exactly the same in all parts; the voice-leading and use of suspension dissonance vary considerably. Even in the *Missa secundi toni* where nine of its thirteen sections show an authentic cadence on the first degree of the scale, there are not two cadences exactly the same. The other Masses exhibit the same diversity in cadences.

5. DISSONANCE TREATMENT

This chapter is an examination of the dissonance treatment in the first four Masses of the *Missarum liber primus*. These procedures were adopted:

1. Each measure was examined for passing and ornamental dissonance (dissonance as a secondary phenomenon). These dissonances were classified according to their melodic movement and rhythm, and in some cases according to function.

2. Each measure was examined for suspension dissonance (dissonance as a primary phenomenon). These dissonances were classified as to structure (vertical) and function (horizontal).

Dissonance as a Secondary Phenomenon

Passing and Auxiliary Dissonances.—In these Masses there are few instances of the minim as a passing note. Example 1 shows a passing

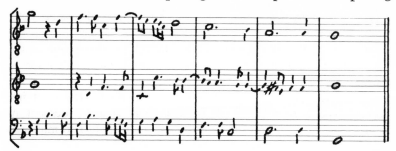

Ex. 1. I Sanctus, 89.

note of the seventh which is a part of a closing cadence. It leads to a clear-cut suspension dissonance, followed by an ornamental resolution. Dissonance rising from ascending movement in minims is found five times in III Sanctus, the result of the imitation of the minim figure seen in the tenor (Ex. 2).

Unaccented semiminim passing notes, ascending and descending, are so abundant that they are to be found on just about every page. Measure 2 of Ex. 2 shows one example in the diminution of the minim figure in the second tenor. Unaccented fusas are also relatively common.

Auxiliary (returning) dissonances.—These are very common in the late Renaissance. The conditions for their use are that they

Ex. 2. III Sanctus, 59.

must come from a consonant note and return to the same note. They must also appear only on the unaccented beats. Example 3 shows one of the 123 found in the Masses. Of these, only three upper dissonant returning notes were found. One is shown in Ex. 4.

Unaccented passing and returning notes.—By far the most important type is seen in Ex. 5. In this, there is a 4-3 descent in semiminims turning upward to a minim (or more). The minim is

Ex. 3. I Kyrie, 44.   Ex. 4. I Gloria, 64.

53

usually part of a suspension dissonance. This figure is found frequently except in the *Missa ad canones,* where only a few instances
were noted. Palestrina's *Missa ad fugam,* which bears a close re-
semblance to Soriano's canon Mass, also shows no passing dissonance of this type. Example 6 shows one of the returning notes
employing the fusa. Several places were noted where the 4-3
is paired with 2-1 in the lowest voice, again leading into a suspension (Ex. 7).

Ex. 5. I Kyrie, 38.   Ex. 6. II Gloria, 57.   Ex. 7. I Goria, 30.

The next two examples help to illustrate the reasons why these
dissonances were permitted in the first place (Ex. 8 and 9). When
the dissonance on this unaccented beat is introduced in conjunct
motion after a preceding accented minim, one expects the dissonating note to be of minim duration; but when it moves conjunctly
to a consonance, it has the psychological effect of a grace note.[1]

Ex.   8.   I Gloria, 107.   Ex.   9.   III Sanctus, 106.

1. Jeppesen, *The Style of Palestrina and the Dissonance,* p. 140.

Example 10a shows the 7-6 semiminim dissonance on the second beat of the measure. The semiminim movement on the second half of the beat also results in a dissonance, but the unaccented portion of any beat is given considerable freedom to assure smooth voice-leading. The general rule for dissonance treatment here is that the voice proceed by step in the same direction, except in the case of

Ex. 10a. IV Sanctus, 42.

returning notes and the cambiata figure. The same type of passing figure with a 4-3 dissonance is also frequent.

Another frequent melodic figure of the late Renaissance is a four-semiminim descending-scale passage beginning on the odd beat. The usual practice is to have the third semiminim consonant, but occasionally the second and third semiminims appear as dis-

Ex. 10b. III Gloria, 56.   Ex. 11. I Kyrie, 54.

55

sonances just before a suspension. (Ex. 10b). Renaissance theorists make no special rule as to the dissonance treatment at such points. In practice, the first two notes of the figure can be a consonance followed by either an unaccented passing dissonance or two consonances. The note following this figure always moves upward by step.

Most music of the period will show frequent use of the cambiata which can be described as "a figure which arises when an unaccented dissonant quarter [semiminim], introduced by step from above, instead of continuing the conjunct motion downward, makes a skip of a third downward and is followed by a step of a second upward, thus reaching the tone of resolution, although late."[2]

Bellermann's investigation of the *nota cambiata* points out that the sixteenth century was the high point for the changing note: "Wir haben oben gesehen, dass sie Palestrina sehr vielfach anwendete, eben so Orlando Lassus—aber auch andere Componisten dieser Zeit, sowohl bedeutendere als auch unbedeutendere, z. B. Clemens non Papa, Jacob Handl, Asola, Hassler, Vittoria, Nanini, Anerio u. A., machten von ihr Gebrauch."[3]

Investigation of Soriano's Masses shows that when he has a voice descend a fourth from an accented to an unaccented minim, he often fills out the interval with a fusa pair in order to avoid the cambiata (Ex. 11). This is turned into a melodic figure in the first and third Masses in the book. In the first four Masses, only four authentic cambiata figures were counted; while this comprises one small segment of Soriano's total output, a search through his Passions according to Matthew and John failed to turn up a single one. The arrangement of the *Marcellus Mass* shows that twelve cambiata figures from the model are eliminated through the change of the vocal line. From the evidence at hand, this appears to be a Renaissance idiom which Soriano did not favor.

The anticipation dissonance is also one of the standard forms of musical embellishment in contrapuntal writing. It appears in descending movement only in the Masses of Soriano where it is usually employed before a suspension dissonance and as an ornamental resolution of a suspension (Ex. 12).

---

2. Jeppesen, *Counterpoint*, p. 32.
3. Heinrich Bellermann, "Die Wechselnote oder Cambiata bei den Componisten des sechszehnten Jahrhunderts," p. 393.

The so-called "consonant fourth" is another Renaissance idiom found frequently in these Masses. It is introduced by step on the weak beat over a stationary bass tone. The fourth is then tied over to the next strong beat, where it is changed into a stronger dissonance but finally makes a regular resolution on the next weak

Ex. 12.   I Gloria, 56.

beat (Ex. 13). As seen in this example, the fourth occasionally appears as a passing note without the sixth. The conjunct movement of the fourth is standard in the late sixteenth century, though earlier composers in the time of Obrecht occasionally approached the fourth by skip. The following example is typical of the "consonant fourth" idiom found in the Masses of Soriano (Ex. 14). Here the sixth is usually present.

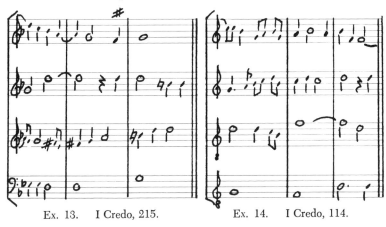

Ex. 13.   I Credo, 215.   Ex. 14.   I Credo, 114.

The majority of the instances cited take place in a cadence formula of the $\left\{ \begin{smallmatrix} 6 & 5 \\ 4 & 3 \end{smallmatrix} \right.$ rhythmic pattern which is characteristic of this type. An example of this formula in semiminim movement was also found (Ex. 15). This was not uncommon practice and appears fairly often in the works of Palestrina. Example 16 is a variation of

Ex. 15.   IV Agnus Dei II, 10.   Ex. 16.   IV Credo, 120.

the consonant fourth idiom in semiminim movement or a "consonant seventh," also frequent in the period.

Example 17 shows the formation of a six-four chord on the second beat of the measure, but instead of passing to a consonant combination, it forms another dissonant chord on the third beat of the measure. This is resolved on the fourth beat of the measure, so that the progression can be considered as another variation of the

Ex. 17.   I Agnus, 7.   Ex. 18.   I Credo, 13.

consonant fourth idiom. In Ex. 18, an instance is noted where Soriano allows the six-four combination after a six-five suspension and then resolves it to a consonant chord. All examples of this type occur over a stationary bass.

Another passing dissonance related to the consonant fourth idiom is the $\frac{6}{5}$ combination introduced on a weak beat following a consonant chord. The dissonating notes are sustained over the next strong beat, while the bass and other voices change position to form another dissonance, a $\frac{4}{3}$ in each case. Nine examples were found in the first four Masses, and in all but one there is a clear-cut function for the $\frac{6}{5}$ passing chord. As seen in Ex. 19, the function

Ex. 19.   II Gloria, 42.

is one of II $\frac{6}{5}$, but the composer chooses to delay the resolution until the first beat of the next measure. Thus, the $\frac{6}{5}$ is introduced followed by $\frac{8\,-}{5\,-}_{4\,3}$ on the second half of the measure.

DISSONANCE AS A PRIMARY PHENOMENON

In the first four Masses of Soriano, the suspension dissonance shows the common practice of the late Renaissance. The most frequent type is the 4-3 (412 times), about three times greater than the 7-6 type (135 times). Almost equal in frequency with the 7-6 is the $\frac{6\,5}{4\,3}$ which has 132 appearances. The 9-8 (or 2-1) and the $\frac{6}{5}$ are equal in number with fifty each. The remaining combinations will be discussed separately.

The term "suspension dissonance" should not be understood to mean that a suspension dissonance must have a tied note from the note of preparation to the dissonance on the strong beat. Occasionally, Soriano uses a disconnected $\smile^{6\,5}_{4\,3}$ in deference to text declamation (Ex. 20 and 21). All necessary considerations of a suspension are otherwise observed. Example 22 demonstrates the fourth in combination with the seventh, and because the fourth is in the upper part, the resolution is apparently staggered to avoid parallel

Ex. 20.　I Credo, 45.

fifths. The fifth combined with the seventh is also frequently found (Ex. 23). The short chain of suspensions beginning with the first beat is most effective as one of the approaches to the consonant fourth combination.

A more complex clash occurs in Ex. 24 where a $^7_{\substack{6\\5}}$ combination appears, but each voice is correctly treated in relationship to the other voices, and the resolution is according to the rules of good

Ex. 21.　I Agnus, 19.

voice-leading. The 4-3 without a fifth above is not too common and appears usually in two- or three-voice sections. The fourth always resolves to the third by step and never moves up to the fifth (Ex. 25). As noted above, the most frequent suspension dissonance is

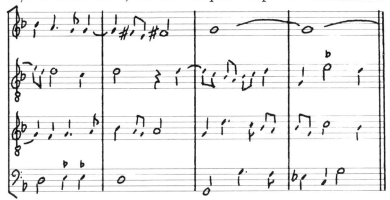

Ex. 22.   I Gloria, 112.

the $_{4\,3}^{5}$ type (Ex. 26). The suspensions of 9-8 or 2-1 are rather common in the four Masses. Examples 27 and 28 are two of the fifty observed. One factor here shows Soriano's predilection for spacious chords; of these fifty, only two are of the 2-1 variety, the rest are 9-8 or 16-15.

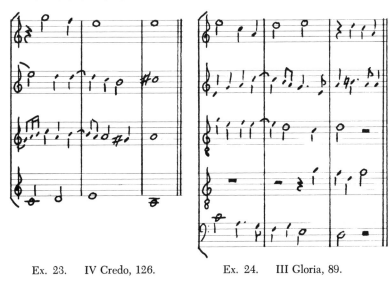

Ex. 23.   IV Credo, 126.   Ex. 24.   III Gloria, 89.

The 2-1 suspension does appear in more complex arrangements as seen in Ex. 29 and 30, but in both cases it is a companion to a fourth and resolves at the same time.

Another favorite device of Renaissance composers is the place-

Ex. 25. I Sanctus, 86.   Ex. 26. II Agnus, 25.

ment of the syncopated second in the lowest voice, which consequently resolves into a third (Ex. 31). In these Masses, the figure is evenly distributed between open and closed position. The $\underset{4\;3}{6-}$ type of resolution (Ex. 32 and 33) is rare, and though it was one of the favored forms of the fifteenth century, it was gradually being

Ex. 27. III Sanctus, 31.   Ex. 28. III Credo, 115.

discarded towards the end of the Renaissance. It usually appears on the second degree of the scale.

The most common is the $\smile^{6}_{4}{}^{5}_{3}$ which resolves with or without ornamental resolution (Ex. 34 and 35). The bass usually ap-

Ex. 29. I Credo, 149.   Ex. 30. III Credo, 113.   Ex. 31. I Gloria, 12.

proaches the chord by a skip up a fourth or down a fifth. Example 34 involves no skip after the resolution, but Ex. 35 shows a strong intermediate cadence from the fifth degree of the scale to the first. Often, when the six-four chord is found on the fifth degree of the scale, the bass moves up a step, forming a false cadence. Example 36 shows a clear case of this type plus the final cadence.

In the works of Palestrina, when the bass moves down a third, a six-three chord often occurs on the new bass note. Haydon notes

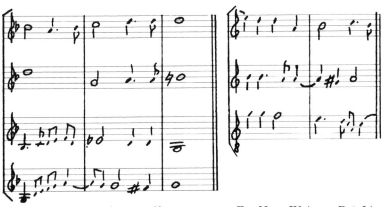

Ex. 32.   II Sanctus, 40.   Ex. 33.   IV Agnus Dei, 24.

Ex. 34.   I Kyrie, 6.   Ex. 35.   I Kyrie, 55.

Ex. 36.   I Kyrie, 21.   Ex. 37.   I Gloria, 29.

Ex. 38.   I Credo, 75.   Ex. 39.   IV Credo, 11.

that this could be regarded as a variation of the progression in which the bass moves up a fourth or down a fifth.[4] In the Masses of Soriano, the same progression is frequently used but characteristically fills out the third with a passing seventh (Ex. 37). The fifteenth-century practice where the bassus and tenor cross during the resolution of the six-four chord appears several times (Ex. 38). One instance is found where the $\smile{}^{6\,5}_{4\,3}$ takes place on the fourth

Ex. 40.   III Kyrie, 37.

degree of the scale, followed by a V-I movement in the bassus (Ex. 39).

More common is the effect of a progression without movement actually taking place in the bass. It simply drops out, and one of the upper voices, usually the tenor, supplies the assumed skip upwards of a fourth (Ex. 40). In the example given below, additional strength is given to the progression by the passing seventh in the altus. Other times the $\smile{}^{6\,5}_{4\,3}$ is followed by a step down in the bass, almost in fauxbourdon procedure (Ex. 41).

Another approach to the six-four chord and the subsequent resolution is shown in Ex. 42. The fourth is properly prepared and resolves downward by step, but the sixth is seen as a passing semiminim in ascending motion. A possible alternative would have been for Soriano to have paused on the sixth step and resolved it

4. Glen Haydon, *The Evolution of the Six-Four Chord*, p. 65.

with the fourth, but in this case, the melodic line takes precedence over a suspension which shows the freedom given to the sixth. In Ex. 43 the fourth seems to be an ascending passing note, but the dissonance is prepared in that the bassus and tenor suspend.

Ex. 41.   III Kyrie, 10.

The most frequent resolution of the six-five syncope comes where the six sustains, the fifth descends stepwise, and the chord changes as a result of movement of the bass. Example 44 shows this chord used as part of a large cadential figure. Five instances

Ex. 42.   IV Kyrie, 52.

were found which show resolutions from the six-five chord to the six-four (Ex. 45). This is followed by a five-three which gives a strong cadential effect without the bass moving. A final example shows a single instance found where the sixth resolves at the same

Ex. 43.   IV Agnus Dei II, 9.

time as the other voices (Ex. 46). A new chord of the sixth is formed on the unaccented beat and leads into a seventh chord suspension. This is followed by a consonant fourth, and leads to a $\smile^5_4$ over the bar line. The resolution follows on the second beat of meas. 9.

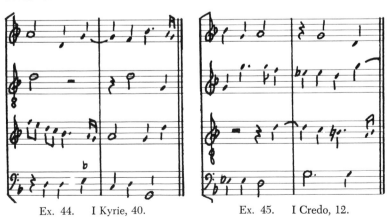

Ex. 44.   I Kyrie, 40.   Ex. 45.   I Credo, 12.

Ex. 46.   IV Agnus II, 5.

6. SUMMARY

The picture of Francesco Soriano as a person and composer emerges a little more clearly through the study of his life and this one book of Masses. As a youth he was fortunate enough to be noticed by Palestrina, and his association with the circle around the great master places him in the highest circles of church music in Rome. The only questionable incident in his career is the period at Mantua, where there seems to have been some dissatisfaction on the part of the Duke. It is worth repeating, however, that the records are most careful to show that Soriano left the position because he wanted to and not because he was dismissed.

At Rome he served as music director in the major churches until he received the coveted position as *maestro di cappella* of St. Peter's where he remained until his retirement. A survey of the total output of his works shows not nearly as many as Palestrina, Byrd, or Lassus, but when compared to his contemporaries in Rome, it shows about the same amount.

The Masses are for the most part in the tradition of the period. Six of the eight are either a parody of a composition by Palestrina or show the same parody material Palestrina used. The *Missa octave tone* has no known model and seems to be based on plain-chant, and the *Missa secundi toni* is a free Mass which uses the *passamezzo moderno* as a head motive.

The first four Masses in the book have been termed parody, but Soriano's procedures are such that one could describe these Masses as having a paraphrase-like treatment of their subject. The *Missa super voces musicales* is an admirable example of a technique that was outdated, but occasional modern touches in this work, such as degree inflection, show him to be abreast of the times. The arrangement of the *Marcellus Mass* expands the model by two voices, resulting in a Mass for double chorus. Soriano remains faithful to the model except for several sections in the Sanctus.

A study of the melodic treatment puts Soriano firmly in the Palestrina tradition. All of the usual intervals are observed with the exception of the skip from a fusa pair. The well-balanced melodic line is typical in the Masses, along with the type of melody with an under-point and the plain-chant type. In several instances, Soriano uses a melodic sequence, something normally considered outside of the style. At the semiminim level and below, Soriano tends to present a more active polyphonic picture than Palestrina, usually in figures of an ornamental character.

Polyphonic procedures are typical of the period. Soriano uses just about every technique available in the period with the exception of extensive homophonic sections, a style of writing which he generally avoids in his Masses. We find single-subject imitation, double subjects, imitation around a *cantus firmus,* canon, and extensive exploitation of voice-groupings. Many sections could be considered in free style, but Soriano usually includes fragments of familiar material from the model.

Dissonance treatment follows the common practice of the period. One outstanding characteristic of Soriano's dissonance treatment was his sparing use of the cambiata figure. Bellermann noted that this was an idiom used frequently by Palestrina and then goes on to list other composers in the same period who also made frequent use of the figure, but Soriano's name is absent from the list. We can only conclude that this was a figure which Soriano did not particularly favor.

APPENDIX

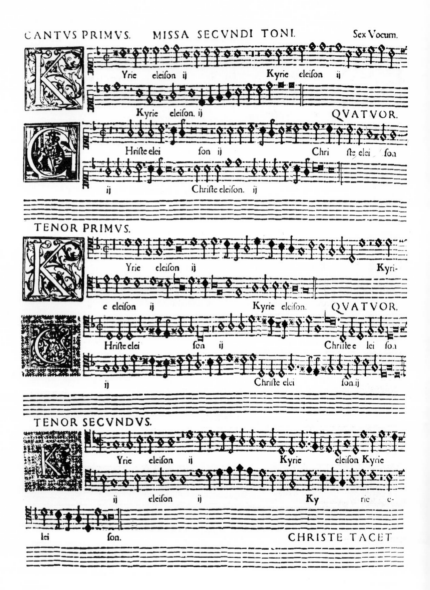

Plate III. Francesco Soriano. *Missa secundi toni.* Kyrie eleison. Christe eleison.

Plate 1V. Francesco Soriano. *Missa secundi toni.* Kyrie eleison. Christe eleison.

FRANCESCO SORIANO
Kyrie from *Missa secondi toni*

Kyrie (*continued*)

Kyrie (*continued*)

Kyrie (*continued*)

Kyrie (*continued*)

Kyrie (*concluded*)

BIBLIOGRAPHY

Ambros, August Wilhelm. *Geschichte der Musik*. 4 vol. Leipzig: F. E. C. Leuckart, 1909.

Analecta hymnica medii aevi. Ed. G. M. Dreves, C. Blume, and H. M. Bannister. 55 vols. Leipzig: 1886-1923.

Andrews, H. K. *An Introduction to the Style of Palestrina*. London: Novello and Co., 1958.

Antiphonale Missarum. Sacra Congregatio Rituum. Romae: Desclée et Socii, 1935.

Apel, Willi. *Gregorian Chant*. Bloomington: Indiana University Press, 1958.

————. *Harvard Dictionary of Music*. Cambridge: Harvard University Press, 1953.

————. *The Notation of Polyphonic Music*, 4th ed., revised with commentary. Cambridge, Mass.: The Mediaeval Academy of America, 1953.

Baini, Giuseppe. *Memorie storico—Critiche della vita e delle opera di Giovanni Pierluigi da Palestrina*, 2 vols. Roma: Della Società Tipografica, 1828.

Baker's Biographical Dictionary of Musicians, 5th ed., revised by Nicolas Slonimsky. New York: G. Schirmer, 1958.

Bellermann, Heinrich. "Die Wechselnote oder Cambiata bei den Componisten des sechszehnten Jahrhunderts," *Allgemeine Musikalische Zeitung* (1869), 385, 393.

Bordes, C., *et al.* (eds.). *Anthologie des maîtres religieux primitifs*. Paris: Société de musique religieuse, 1893-95.

Brenet, Michel [Marie Bobillier]. *Palestrina*. Paris: Librairie Félix Alcan, 1919.

Bukofzer, Manfred. *Music in the Baroque Era*. New York: W. W. Norton, 1947.

Cametti, Alberto. *Cenni biografici di Giovanni Pierluigi da Palestrina*. Milano: G. Ricordi & Co. [1895].

————. *Palestrina*. Milano: Bottega di Poesia, 1925.

Casimiri, Raphael (ed.) *Missa Cantantibus Organis*. Romae: Pontificum Institutum Musicae Sacrae, 1930.

Celani, Enrico. "I Cantori della Cappella Pontifica nei secoli xvi-xvii," *Rivista Musicale Italiana*, XVI (1907), 82-104, 752-90.

Coates, Henry. *Palestrina*. London: J. M. Dent & Sons, Ltd., 1948.

Eitner, Robert. *Biographisch-bibliographisches Quellen-Lexikon der Musiker und Musikgelehrten der christlichen Zeitrechnung bis zur Mitte des 19. Jahrhunderts*. Leipzig: Breitkopf & Härtel, 1898.

Fellerer, Gustav. *The History of Catholic Church Music*. Trans. Francis A. Brunner. Baltimore: Helicon Press, 1961.

————. *Palestrina: Leben und Werke*. Düsseldorf: Musikverlag Schwann, 1960.

Festa, Constantius. *Hymni per Totum Annum*. Transcripsit et curavit Glen Haydon. Romae: Pontificum Institutum Musicae Sacrae, 1958.

Fétis, François Joseph. *Biographie universelle des musiciens et bibliographie générale de la musique*. 8 vols. Paris: Firmin-Didot, 1883-84.

Fux, Johann Joseph. *Steps to Parnassus*. Trans. and ed. Alfred Mann with the collaboration of John St. Edmunds. New York: W. W. Norton, 1943.

Grout, Donald Jay. *A History of Western Music*. New York: W. W. Norton, 1960.

Grove's Dictionary of Music and Musicians, 5th ed. Ed. Eric Blom. London: Macmillan and Co., Ltd., 1954.

Haberl, Francis X. "Das Archiv der Gonzaga in Mantua," *Kirchenmusikalisches Jahrbuch*, I (1886), 31-41.

————. "Hieronymus Frescobaldi," *Kirchenmusikalisches Jahrbuch*, II (1887), 67-82.

————. "Lebensgang und Werke des Francesco Soriano," *Kirchenmusikalisches Jahrbuch*, X (1895), 95-103.

————. "Responsoria Chori ad Cantus Passionis D. N. J. Christe," *Kirchenmusikalisches Jahrbuch*, X (1895), 1-24.

————. "Die römische 'schola cantorum' und die päpstlichen Kapellsänger bis zur Mitte des 16. Jahrhunderts," *Vierteljahrsschrift für Musikwissenschaft*, VII (1897), 189-296.

————. "Thomas Luca Victoria," *Kirchenmusikalisches Jahrbuch*, XI (1896), 72-84.

Haydon, Glen. *The Evolution of the Six-Four Chord: A Chapter in the History of Dissonance Treatment*. Berkeley: University of California Press, 1933.

Jeppesen, Knud. *Counterpoint*. Trans. with Introduction, Glen Haydon. Englewood Cliffs, N.J.: Prentice-Hall, 1939.

————. "The Recently Discovered Mantova Masses of Palestrina," *Acta Musicologica*, XXII (1950), 36-47.

————. *The Style of Palestrina and the Dissonance*, 2nd ed. Trans. Margaret Homerick, Copenhagen: Ejnar Munksgaard, 1946.

Julian, John. *A Dictionary of Hymnology*, 2 vols. New York: Dover Publications, 1907.

Kast, Paul. "Francesco Soriano," *Die Musik in Geschichte und Gegenwart*. Ed. Friedrich Blume. Vol. XII, cols. 391-94.

Kinsky, Georg. "Schriftstücke aus dem Palestrina Kreis," *Peter Wagner Festschrift*. Leipzig: Breitkopf & Härtel, 1926, 108-17.

Kirnberger, Johann Phil. *Die Kunst des reinen Satzes in der Musik*. Berlin & Königsberg: G. J. Decker & G. L. Hartung, 1774.

Krieg, Franz. *Katholische Kirchenmusik*. Teufen: Verlag Arthur Niggli & Willy Verkauf, 1954.

Liber Usualis. Tournai: Desclée et Cie., 1947.

Lowinsky, Edward E. *Tonality and Atonality in Sixteenth-Century Music*. Berkeley: University of California Press, 1961.

Moliter, P. Raphael. *Die nach-tridentinische Choral-Reform zu Rom*, 2 vol. Leipzig: F. E. C. Leuckart, 1901.

Morris, R. O. *Contrapuntal Technique in the Sixteenth Century*. Oxford: Clarendon Press, 1922.

Moser, Hans Joachim. *Musik Lexikon*, 4th ed., revised. Hamburg: Musikverlag Hans Sikorski, 1955.

————. "Vestiva i colli," *Archiv für Musikforschung*, IV (1939), 129-56.

Nikel, Emil. *Geschichte der katholischen Kirchenmusik*. Breslau: Verlag von Franz Goerlich, 1908.

O'Connell, J. B. (trans.). *Sacred Music and Liturgy; Instruction of the Sacred Congregation of Rites Concerning Sacred Music and Sacred Liturgy in Accordance with the Encyclical Letters of Pope Pius XII, Sacra disciplina*. Westminster, Md.: The Newman Press [1959].

Palestrina, Giovanni Pierluigi. *Le Opera Complete*. Ed. Raffaele Casimiri. Roma: Edizione Fratelli Scalera, 1939.

————. *Werke*. 33 vols. Ed. Theodor de Witt, Franz Commer, Franz Espagne, Franz Xaver Haberl. Leipzig: Breitkopf & Härtel, 1874-1907.

Pfatteicher, Carl F., and Dudley Fitts (eds.). *Office Hymns of the Church*. Boston: McLaughlin & Reilly Co., 1951.

Porter, Father Thomas E., S.J. Personal interview, March 19, 1964.

Proske, Carl. *Missa Papae Marcelli triplici concentu distincta didelicet.* Mainz: 1850.

———— (ed.). *Selectus novus missarum praestantissimorum superioris aevi auctorum, justa codices originales.* Ratisbonae: F. Pustet, 1855-59.

Reese, Gustave. *Music in the Middle Ages.* New York: W. W. Norton, 1940.

————. *Music in the Renaissance,* revised ed. New York: W. W. Norton, 1959.

Riemann Musik Lexikon, 3 vols., 12th ed., revised by Wilibald Gurlitt. Mainz: B. Schotts Söhne, 1959.

Rore, Cipriani. *Opera Omnia.* Ed. Bernhardus Meier. Rome: American Institute of Musicology, 1961.

Ruhnke, Martin. "Hexachord," *Die Musik in Geschichte und Gegenwart.* Ed. Friedrich Blume. Vol. VI, cols. 352-58.

Sachs, Curt. *Rhythm and Tempo.* New York: W. W. Norton, 1953.

Schmidl, Carlo. *Dizionario universale dei musicisti,* 3 vols. Milan: Casa Editrice Sonzogno, 1937-38.

Schuler, Rev. Richard J. "The Roman Choirs," *Caecilia,* LXXXIV (1957), 345-54.

Sparks, Edgar H. *Cantus Firmus in Mass and Motet, 1420-1520.* Berkeley: University of California Press, 1963.

Strunk, Oliver. *Source Readings in Music History.* New York: W. W. Norton, 1950.

Tinctoris, Johannis. *The Art of Counterpoint.* Trans. and ed. Albert Seay. American Institute of Musicology, 1961.

Torchi, Luigi (ed.). *L'Arte musicale in Italia,* 7 vols. Milano: G. Ricordi, 1897.

Victoria, Thomas Ludovici. *Opera Omnia.* Ed. Philippe Pedrell. Leipzig: Breitkopf & Härtel, 1913.

Vogel, Emil. *Bibliothek der gedruckten weltlichen Vokalmusik Italiens, 1500-1700.* Berlin: A. Haack, 1892.

Wagner, Peter. *Geschichte der Messe.* Leipzig: Breitkopf & Härtel, 1913.

Ward, John. "Passamezzo," *Die Musik in Geschichte und Gegenwart.* Ed. Friedrich Blume. Vol. X, cols. 877-80.

Yates Hadley. "A History of the Cadence in Polyphonic Music through the Fifteenth Century." Ph.D. dissertation, Indiana University, 1962.

Zimmermann, F. X. *Die Kirchen Roms.* München: R. Piper & Co., 1935.

UNIVERSITY OF FLORIDA MONOGRAPHS

Humanities

No. 1: *Uncollected Letters of James Gates Percival*, edited by Harry R. Warfel

No. 2: *Leigh Hunt's Autobiography: The Earliest Sketches*, edited by Stephen F. Fogle.

No. 3: *Pause Patterns in Elizabethan and Jacobean Drama*, by Ants Oras

No. 4: *Rhetoric and American Poetry of the Early National Period*, by Gordon E. Bigelow

No. 5: *The Background of The Princess Casamassima*, by W. H. Tilley

No. 6: *Indian Sculpture in the John and Mable Ringling Museum of Art*, by Roy C. Craven, Jr.

No. 7: *The Cestus. A Mask*, edited by Thomas B. Stroup

No. 8: *Tamburlaine, Part I, and Its Audience*, by Frank B. Fieler

No. 9: *The case of John Darrell: Minister and Exorcist*, by Corinne Holt Rickert

No. 10: *Reflections of the Civil War in Southern Humor*, by Wade H. Hall

No. 11: *Charles Dodgson, Semeiotician*, by Daniel F. Kirk

No. 12: *Three Middle English Religious Poems*, edited by R. H. Bowers

No. 13: *The Existentialism of Miguel de Unamuno*, by José Huertas-Jourda

No. 14: *Four Spiritual Crises in Mid-Century American Fiction*, by Robert Detweiler

No. 15: *Style and Society in German Literary Expressionism*, by Egbert Krispyn

No. 16: *The Reach of Art: A Study in the Prosody of Pope*, by Jacob H. Adler

No. 17: *Malraux, Sartre, and Aragon as Political Novelists*, by Catharine Savage

No. 18: *Las Guerras Carlistas y el Reinado Isabelino en la Obra de Ramón del Valle-Inclán*, por María Dolores Lado

No. 19: *Diderot's Vie de Sénèque: A Swan Song Revised*, by Douglas A. Bonneville

No. 20: *Blank Verse and Chronology in Milton*, by Ants Oras

No. 21: *Milton's Elisions*, by Robert O. Evans

No. 22: *Prayer in Sixteenth-Century England*, by Faye L. Kelly

No. 23: *The Strangers: The Tragic World of Tristan L'Hermite*, by Claude K. Abraham

No. 24: *Dramatic Uses of Biblical Allusion in Marlowe and Shakespeare*, by James H. Sims

No. 25: *Doubt and Dogma in Maria Edgeworth*, by Mark D. Hawthorne

No. 26: *The Masses of Francesco Soriano*, by S. Philip Kniseley